Praise for Raising the Dust

"Such a concise, instructive resource! Allison and Welsh outline the philosophy, principles, process, and practices of establishing and deepening the diaconates, and what they have to say here deserves careful consideration. After all, healthy churches have healthy diaconates."

Dr. Matthew Arbo, Assistant Professor of Biblical and Theological Studies at Oklahoma Baptist University

"Our world needs love and selfless service — and church leaders who can lead the way in those selfless acts. Gregg and Ryan have written a book that tangibly helps the church understand the importance of deacons in accomplishing our call to be communities of service and love for the life of the world. We look forward to using this book in our churches."

Tyler Johnson, Lead Pastor at Redemption Church, AZ

"It is easy to recognize how important pastoral leadership is for the local church. In this book, Allison and Welsh provide a biblical guide for understanding the importance of the overall structure of church leadership, and in particular the crucial role that a deacon ministry plays in a healthy church. This book will serve churches well as a guide for understanding a biblical perspective on the responsibilities of deacons and for developing a healthy deacon ministry."

Ken Magnuson, Professor of Christian Ethics, The Southern Baptist Theological Seminary

"This book challenges churches to rethink, both theologically and practically, the ministry of deacons, which seems to have been diminished within churches today. Gregg and Ryan call us to 'wake up' and be responsible through the biblical mandate for the church as it relates to the office of deacons. As a youth pastor of 40+ years, along with being a pastor of discipleship, I believe that the principles shared in this book will have long-lasting impact for God's family."

Steve Keels, Executive Pastor of Discipleship, Good
Shepherd Community Church, Boring, Oregon

"A healthy church is dependent on servant leadership. Allison and Welsh remind us that the diaconate is an essential part of how a healthy church functions by clarifying the theology and practice of the diaconate. Churches looking to equip the saints for the work of ministry should start with this resource."

J. T. English III, Institute Pastor, The Village Church

"The church often sits atop a rich field of untapped resources while fretting about the challenges and demands of ministry. The role of deacon in the church is a much-neglected opportunity to honor and inspire some of the most faithful and gifted saints in our body. Allison and Welsh wisely remind us of this treasure and give us practical wisdom for developing and unleashing this latent potential in the church."

Brad House, Executive Pastor, Sojourn Community
Church, Louisville, KY, and author of *Community:
Taking Your Small Groups Off Life Support*

"Gregg and Ryan do churches a great service with this biblically founded practical manual for deacons. It comes in a context of an excellent theology of church leadership and years of hands on experience."

Gerry Breshears, PhD, Professor of Theology Western Seminary, Portland

"The Sojourn Network 'How-To' books are a great combination of biblical theology and practical advice, driven by a commitment to the gospel and the local congregation. Written by the local church for the local church — just the job!"

>**Tim Chester**, pastor of Grace Church Boroughbridge,
>faculty member of Crosslands Training, and author
>of over 40 books

"This series brings pastoral wisdom for everyday life in the church of Jesus Christ. Think of these short, practical books as the equivalent of a healthy breakfast, a sandwich and apple for lunch, and a family enjoying dinner together. The foundational theology is nutritious, and the practical applications will keep the body strong."

>**Dr. David Powlison**, Executive Director of CCEF;
>senior editor, Journal of Biblical Counseling; author
>of *Good and Angry: Redeeming Anger* and *Making All
>Things New: Restoring Joy to the Sexually Broken*

"Most leaders don't need another abstract book on leadership; we need help with the 'how-to's.' And my friends in the Sojourn Network excel in this area. I've been well served by their practical ministry wisdom, and I know you will be too."

>**Bob Thune**, Founding Pastor, Coram Deo Church,
>Omaha, NE, author of *Gospel Eldership* and co-
>author of *The Gospel-Centered Life*

"I cannot express strong enough what a valuable resource this is for church planters, church planting teams and young churches. The topics that are addressed in these books are so needed in young churches. I have been in ministry and missions for over 30 years and I learned a lot from reading. Very engaging and very practical!"

Larry McCrary, Co-Founder and Director of The
Upstream Collective

"There are many aspects of pastoral ministry that aren't (and simply can't) be taught in seminary. Even further, many pastors simply don't have the benefit of a brotherhood of pastors that they can lean on to help them navigate topics such as building a healthy plurality of elders or working with artists in the church. I'm thankful for the men and women who labored to produce this series, which is both theologically-driven and practically-minded. The Sojourn Network "How-To" series is a great resource for pastors and church planters alike."

Jamaal Williams, Lead Pastor of Sojourn Midtown,
Louisville, KY

"HOW-TO" EQUIP DEACONS
TO SERVE THE CHURCH

Raising
THE
DUST

Gregg Allison & Ryan Welsh

Series Editor: Dave Harvey

Raising the Dust
"How-To" Equip Deacons to Serve the Church

© 2019 Gregg Allison and Ryan Welsh
All rights reserved.

A publication of Sojourn Network Press in Louisville, KY. For more books by Sojourn Network, visit us at sojournnetwork.com/store.

A few sections of this book have been adapted with permission from Gregg Allison and John S. Feinberg's book, *Sojourners and Strangers: The Doctrine of the Church* (Wheaton: Crossway, 2012).

Cover design: Josh Noom & Benjamin Vrbicek
Interior design: Benjamin Vrbicek

Trade paperback ISBN: 978-1732055285

The Sojourn Network book series is dedicated to the pastors, elders, and deacons of Sojourn Network churches. Because you are faithful, the church will be served and sent as we plant, grow, and multiply healthy churches that last.

CONTENTS

The Word
The Office
The Qualifications
The Gender
The Responsibilities

What Is the Difference Between Members
    and Deacons?
Should Deacons and Deaconesses Serve in
    Specific Ministries?
Should Deacons and Deaconesses Be Limited in
    What They Can Do?
How Many Deacons Should a Church Have and
    How Long Should They Serve?

The Course of Development
The Transition from Deacon Board to Elder Plurality
The Transition from Deacon to Elder

1. Case Studies
2. Resources for Deacons and Deaconesses
3. Examining Questions for Deacon(ess) Candidates
4. Example Deacon(ess) Development Process

SERIES PREFACE

Why should the Sojourn Network publish a "How-To" series?

It's an excellent question, since it leads to a more personal and pertinent question for you: *Why should you bother to read any of these books?*

Sojourn Network, the ministry I am honored to lead, exists to plant, grow, and multiply healthy networks, churches, and pastors. Therefore, it seems only natural to convert some of our leader's best thinking and practices into written material focusing on the "How-To" aspects of local church ministry and multiplication.

We love church planters and church planting. But we've come to believe it's not enough to do assessments and fund church plants. We must also help, equip, and learn from one another in order to be good shepherds and leaders. We must stir up one another to the good work of leading churches towards their most fruitful future.

That's why some books will lend themselves to soul calibration for ministry longevity, while others will examine the riggings of specific ministries or specialized mission. This is essential work to building ministries *that last*. But God has also placed it on our hearts to share our mistakes and most fruitful practices so that others might improve upon what we have done. This way, everyone wins.

If our prayer is answered, this series will bring thoughtful, pastoral, charitable, gospel-saturated, church-grounded, renewal-based "practice" to the rhythms of local church life and network collaboration.

May these "How-To" guides truly serve you. May they arm you with new ideas for greater leadership effectiveness. Finally, may they inspire you to love Jesus more and serve his people with grace-inspired gladness, in a ministry that passes the test of time.

Dave Harvey
President, Sojourn Network

INTRODUCTORY LETTER

Dear fellow church leader,

We both serve as pastors in local churches, as well as educators in the academic arena. One of us (Gregg) serves full-time as a seminary professor and a lay elder in a local church. The other (Ryan) serves full-time as a lead pastor of a local church and part-time teaching at a university. On a typical day, our full-time service differs from one another. However, as we compare notes and stories, we agree that a deficient ecclesiology is prevalent today in both the local church and the academy. Many pastors ground their leadership model in power and practicality, while many pastors-in-training have a lack of interest in the governance of the church and are far more interested in "sexier" theological studies.

The apostle Paul knew how important godly leadership in the church is for the body of Christ to increase and flourish. He writes what we call his pastoral epistles for just such a reason. But let's be honest, training leaders is difficult and time-consuming. We believe the biggest reason pastors fail to train up leaders in the church is not that they are uninterested, but because it can be a daunting assignment. We believe this small book might be able to assist pastors who feel this way.

There is much to say about church leadership structures and how to train for such. However, this book is intended only to address the role of deacon. Dave Harvey has written a previous book in this series titled *Healthy Plurality = Durable Church*. Dave's book ought to be seen as a precursor to this book because our teaching on the office of deacon in the local church is based on a model where a church is led by a plurality of elders.

This work is not intended for the university or the seminary, but for the local church. Our goal is to briefly outline one level of church leadership — the diaconate — so as to serve local church leaders in equipping and installing deacons and deaconesses for the health of the body of Christ. We seek to accomplish this in four steps by:

- drafting a biblical blueprint for the office of deacon (philosophy)
- asking and answering crucial questions (principles)
- outlining a proper training process (process)
- offering a few brief case studies (practices)

Brothers and sisters in ministry, our prayer is that this book will serve you and your people well. If just one local church is aided by this work in the development of deacons and deaconesses, then it was well worth the work. May we serve our gracious Lord humbly and care for his blood-bought people deeply. We believe that a healthy deacon ministry will help in doing exactly that.

Your partners in gospel ministry,
Gregg & Ryan

PHILOSOPHY

DEACONS AND THEIR ROLES

Deacon (n.) [dee-kuh n]
   Definition: servant
   Etymology: dust raised up by servants

The Word

Words have meaning. Sometimes a range of meaning. However, when its scope becomes too broad, it renders the word unclear at best and obsolete at worst. A contemporary example is the word "awesome." What does it mean? Does it mean anything anymore? What once was understood as the description of a reaction to the astonishing works of God is now used universally. The famous "Everything is Awesome" song from the 2014 Lego movie sufficiently proves the point. If everything is awesome, nothing is awesome. In like manner, the church has overused and misused the word "deacon" to its harm. From a member of a board who makes financial decisions for the church, to the title given to a female who functionally exercises the role of elder but the church refuses to call her such, to the pre-elder title given to a man in elder training, the term "deacon" is misused and abused.

In order to best understand the term "deacon," it is helpful to look at both its etymology and definition. Whereas definition refers to the meaning of a word, etymology refers to its history and origin. Interestingly, the etymology of "deacon" carries the idea of "through the dust." This describes the dust raised by servants who are hard at work. This history paints an accurate picture of the role and calling of those in the diaconate.

At the heart of the term "deacon" and the office — the "diaconate" — is *service*. Deacons are Christians who serve the Lord Jesus by leading ministries in the local church. At times,

> **Deacons are Christians who serve the Lord Jesus by leading ministries in the local church.**

the word commonly translated "deacon" (διάκονος, *diakonos*) is rendered "servant" in Scripture. This generic translation occurs in reference to (1) human government as "God's servant" (Romans 13:4); (2) Christ as "a servant to the circumcised" (Romans 15:8); and (3) false apostles as "servants" of Satan, disguising themselves as "servants of righteousness" (2 Corinthians 11:14–15) rather than as "servants of Christ" (2 Corinthians 11:23).

Paul also uses the word to refer to himself and his coworkers as "servants of God/Christ" (2 Corinthians 6:4; Colossians 1:7; 1 Timothy 4:6) and, thus, ministers of "the church" (Colossians 1:24–25), "servants through whom" others believe in Christ (1 Corinthians 3:5), "ministers of a new covenant" (2 Corinthians 3:6) or of the gospel (Ephesians 3:7; Colossians 1:23). Such servants, as they engage in carrying out God's will and purpose, must be "faithful . . . in the Lord" (Ephesians 6:21; Colossians 4:7).

In sum, this broad usage of the word translated "servant" or "minister" carries the idea of working under, or on behalf of, someone or something. Though a chief tenet of modern secular culture, self-service is nowhere to be found in God's Word. Biblically speaking, no one "serves oneself;" the notion is absurd! Service is always directed toward another. Therefore, we serve God: we act on behalf of the Lord, doing his will as faithful servants. We are ministers commissioned by God, exercising our ministries in, from, and for his church.

The Office

The diaconate, as an office, can be a confusing concept. If deacons are simply servants who aid the church in various ways, then why is it considered an office instead of simply being identified as a part of the whole of the volunteers within the church? Many associate the beginning of the office of deacon with Acts 6:1–6 narrative:

> Now in these days when the disciples were increasing in number, a complaint by the Hellenists arose against the Hebrews because their widows were being neglected in the daily distribution. And the twelve summoned the full number of the disciples and said, "It is not right that we should give up preaching the word of God to serve (διακονέω, *diakonéō*) tables. Therefore,

brothers, pick out from among you seven men of good repute, full of the Spirit and of wisdom, whom we will appoint to this duty. But we will devote ourselves to prayer and to the ministry (διαχονια, *diakonia*) of the word." And what they said pleased the whole gathering, and they chose Stephen, a man full of faith and of the Holy Spirit, and Philip, and Prochorus, and Nicanor, and Timon, and Parmenas, and Nicolaus, a proselyte of Antioch. These they set before the apostles, and they prayed and laid their hands on them.

Whatever one decides about this event — whether or not it is the beginning of the diaconate — we must be cautious about constructing the typical division between the role of elders and the role of deacons. This typical division is stated as follows: "deacons are to be involved in the physical and temporal needs of the church, while elders are to be devoted to spiritual matters." This is too narrow of an understanding. The word "deacon" itself does not determine the nature of the service rendered. In subsequent narratives in the book of Acts, we find two of the "deacons" presented in Acts 6 engaging in activities not typically associated with the office of deacon. Stephen combats the Sanhedrin and condemns the Jewish leaders for executing Jesus, a confrontation for which he is martyred (Acts 6:8–8:3). Also, Philip engages in preaching the gospel to the Samaritans, to the Ethiopian eunuch, and in the towns from Azotus to Caesarea, resulting in widespread conversion to Christ (Acts 8:4–40). These "deacons" were certainly not restricted to serving as table waiters!

In many contemporary churches, the leadership structure is a solo pastor with a board of deacons. In this polity, deacons minister like pastors: they preach, teach, lead, and more. Consequently, in those churches, the diaconate functions like the office of pastor/elder. However, if we explore Scripture, a different pattern of leadership presents itself. A church should be led by a plurality of elders, who are qualified men, and should be served by deacons, who are qualified men and women. In this church structure, deacons are members who serve the Lord Jesus by leading non-elder level ministries of the church. These appointed deacons are not elders, but they are also not simply volunteers. They are faithful and qualified leaders of ministries that range across many areas of service.

The Qualifications

Scripture presents the qualifications of deacons in 1 Timothy 3:8–13:

> Deacons likewise must be dignified, not double-tongued, not addicted to much wine, not greedy for dishonest gain. They must hold the mystery of the faith with a clear conscience. And let them also be tested first; then let them serve as deacons if they prove themselves blameless. Their wives likewise must be dignified, not slanderers, but sober-minded, faithful in all things. Let deacons each be the husband of one wife, managing their children and their own households well. For those who serve well as deacons gain a good

standing for themselves and also great confidence in the faith that is in Christ Jesus.

The basic structure of this passage may be outlined as follows: Paul presents several general characteristics of all servants (vv. 8–10), then offers a brief discussion of women — either wives of deacons or deaconesses (v. 11) — and their qualifications, then turns to household requirements for male deacons (v. 12), and finally concludes with a commendation for all servants of Jesus Christ (v. 13).

This structure directly follows Paul's brief words about elder qualifications (1 Timothy 3:1–7). It is easy to see the similarities of the qualifications of deacons to those of elders. Both groups must be dignified, of noble character, not engaged in duplicitous speech so as to mislead people, have solid family dynamics, embrace sound doctrine, and avoid addictions. As for the qualifications of deacons that are *different* from those of elders, two stand out:

(1) Whereas elders must be able to teach (v. 2), this is not a requirement for deacons, though this certainly does not mean that deacons cannot or do not teach.

(2) Whereas both groups must have managerial abilities, these competencies are used by elders to lead the church (v. 5) while deacons use them to serve the church.

Before being enlisted to serve in the church, deacons must "be tested first; then let them serve as deacons if they prove themselves blameless" (v. 10). This assessment of deacons is directed at both their meeting of the character qualifications and their personal abilities. Dangerously, churches often focus only on the latter evaluation giving little heed to those serving in the diaconate, a neglect that is contrasted by the reward promised to them: "those who serve well as deacons gain a good standing for themselves and also great confidence in the faith that is in Christ Jesus" (v. 13). Often, unfortunately, the qualification requirements for church offices are replaced by urgent pragmatism: enticed by time limitations and human gifting, pastors can harmfully install leaders who are gifted but not qualified.

However, qualified and faithful deacons should enjoy a good standing before the congregation (both elders and members), who are benefited by — and thus are called to respect — the service of deacons. Faithful deacons experience great confidence in their serving ministries, perhaps great assurance before the ultimate servant, Jesus. Lest deacons believe that their service to the church is where their certainty is found, it must be recalled that such certainty is not ultimately rooted in what they do; rather, they are grounded by faith in Christ and what he has done on their behalf.

The Gender

There is great debate today regarding gender restrictions in church leadership. The Bible seems to speak more clearly on gender restrictions for the role of elder in a way that it does not for the role of deacon. In the list of qualifications for deacons, 1 Timothy 3:11 may be interpreted in two conflicting ways. Here is the verse with the key point of debate appearing as the transliteration of the Greek word in the original text: "*gunaikas* likewise must be dignified, not slanderers, but sober-minded, faithful in all things." The two different understandings are: (1) This list of qualifications is for "their wives" (ESV, NIV 1984), that is, the wives of deacons. Along with their deacon-husbands, the wives of deacons must meet certain qualifications. (2) This list of qualifications is for "women" (NASB, NIV 2011), that is, deacons who are women (deaconesses), like their male counterparts, must meet certain (additional) qualifications.

According to the first interpretation, in the midst of his presentation of the qualifications of deacons, who must be men, Paul includes several characteristics that must be true of their wives. At the core of his address may stand the fact that as deacons engage in their service in the church, they are often accompanied by their wives, who must be qualified for this accompanying role. This understanding is shown in church leadership structures in the following ways:

(1a) churches that have one pastor and a board of deacons: in accordance with this interpretation, and because this board functions in ways similar to a group of pastors/elders, only men can be deacons.

(1b) churches that have a plurality of elders and a plurality of deacons: in accordance with this interpretation, and even though there is a clear distinction between elders, who must be men (in accordance with 1 Timothy 2:12–15), and deacons, only men can be deacons.

According to the second interpretation, in the midst of his presentation of the general characteristics of all deacons (vv. 8–10), and prior to his focused discussion of the household requirements for male deacons (v. 12), Paul inserts a brief list of qualifications for female deacons, or deaconesses. These are additional characteristics that must be true for women who serve in the office of deacon. This understanding is shown in church leadership structures in the following ways:

(2a) churches that have one pastor and a board of deacons: in accordance with this interpretation, and because this board is engaged in serving ministries and not in pastoral roles, both men and women can be deacons.

(2b) churches that have a plurality of elders and a plurality of deacons: in accordance with this interpretation, and because there is a clear distinction between elders, who must be men (in accordance with 1 Timothy 2:12–15), and deacons, both men and women can be deacons.

(2c) churches that have both elders and deacons and, not following the traditional interpretation that understands 1 Timothy 2:12–15 as limiting the office of elders to men, permit both men and women to be both elders and deacons (that is, there are no gender restrictions placed on either the pastorate or the diaconate).

Though the first interpretation is plausible, the second is the stronger of the two for multiple reasons. The first reason concerns the function of the word "likewise" in Paul's list of qualifications. Like an elder, who "must be" a certain type of person (1 Timothy 3:2), and like a deacon, who "must be" a certain type of person (v. 8); a female deacon "must be" a certain type of person (v. 11; note that in the original Greek text, the words "must be" are not present, however every translation includes them as they are implied in the context). Thus, Paul first lists the qualifications of elders (vv. 1–7), then lists the general qualifications of deacons (vv. 8–10), using the word "likewise" to indicate that these characteristics "must be" true of all deacons, then lists the specific qualifications of female deacons (v. 11), using the word "likewise" to indicate that these characteristics "must be" true of all deaconesses.

Second, the list in verse 11 is like the other lists that outline the qualifications for a church office. Elders, deacons, and female deacons serve in offices. This tips the interpretation in favor of the second option. Third, had Paul wanted to indicate that he was talking about wives, he could have written "wives of deacons" or "their wives." Note that the ESV does translate verse 11 using the phrase "their wives," but the word "their" is not in the original Greek text; it was supplied by the translators of the ESV, which favors the first interpretation. Fourth and finally, the absence of a list of qualifications for the wives of elders favors the view that Paul is addressing deaconesses. In his discussion of the qualifications of elders (vv. 1–7), Paul does not say anything about their wives and qualifications that these women must meet. It seems strange that Paul would address the wives of deacons but not the wives of elders.

Discerning interpreters will wonder why Paul didn't just write "deaconesses" to be more clear? Interestingly, there was no word for deaconesses in Greek at this time. So he uses the word *gunaikas*, which can mean women or wives. In either case, he does indicate a change in subject matter: either wives of deacons, who must meet certain qualifications along with their husband-deacons, or female deacons, who must meet certain qualifications to serve in the office of deaconess.

Taking the second interpretation as more plausible than the first produces an important point about the accessibility of this office to men and women. Like their male counterparts, deaconesses do not have responsibilities to teach, lead, pray for the sick, and shepherd the church, so they are not violating scriptural injunctions against women being elders/pastors (1 Timothy 2:12–15). Accordingly, option (2b) above seems to be the healthiest church leadership structure:

(2b) churches have a plurality of elders and a plurality of deacons; moreover, because there is a clear distinction between elders, who must be men (in accordance with 1 Timothy 2:12–15), and deacons, both men and women can be deacons.

Thus, the diaconate is accessible to both men and women.

In all deacon(ess) ministries, the assumption is that these ministries are thoroughly grounded on and explicitly saturated with Scripture and sound theology, and that men and women alike follow and teach in accordance with the church's elder-established theology. But because these ministries are not those of the elders — preaching, leading, praying, and shepherding at the highest level of church authority and activity — both deacons and deaconesses may be engaged.

The Responsibilities

One of the most important factors for success in any job is the possession of a thorough job description. Scripture, however, does not provide one for deacons. Rather, it seems to give a general principle: deacons are leading servants in all non-elder level roles within ministries of the church. At this point, one should ask, what are non-elder level roles?

> **Deacons are leading servants in all non-elder level roles within ministries of the church.**

The most suitable way to answer such a question is to ask another: what are the responsibilities of elders?

Elders exercise four roles:

(1) Elders teach (1 Timothy 3:2; 5:17), bearing the responsibility to communicate biblical truth and sound doctrine.

(2) Elders lead (1 Timothy 3:5; 5:17), exercising proper authority, under the headship of Jesus Christ, at the highest level of human governance in the church.

(3) Elders pray (as all Christians are called to do), interceding especially for the sick (James 5:13–16).

(4) Elders shepherd (1 Peter 5:1–4), exercising oversight and exemplifying Christlikeness.

Thus, if elders are responsible for teaching, leading, praying, and shepherding, then deacons are responsible for leading the other, non-elder level ministries of the church: ministries of mercy, women's ministries, men's ministries, hospitality, community groups, kids' ministries, missions, bereavement ministries, and many more. These ministries may — but not necessarily — be led by elders as well. Therefore, deacons and deaconesses are leading servants and possess and exercise the requisite authority for carrying out their responsibilities. They should be deferred to and accorded respect by those within their ministry. Deacon(ess)-level responsibilities include (but are not limited to):

- Community groups: Community groups may be led by a man and a woman who are co-responsible for discipleship, care, and mission. In most cases this will be a husband and a wife, or a single man and a single woman, but it is not restricted to such an arrangement. (Note: Some churches expect and commission their community group leaders to exercise a significant teaching role to both men and women in the group. In this situation, the elders may require the group leaders to be men.)
- Teaching/training activities: Because one of the responsibilities of pastors is to teach the Bible and communicate sound doctrine, elders teach/lead the training in mixed-gender contexts in which those activities are central. In other activities (e.g.,

missions training, care, mercy), deacons and deaconesses may teach/lead the training.

- Worship services: Deacons and deaconesses alike may design, lead, and participate in most aspects of the Sunday liturgy. Teaching and preaching is the one area that is excluded, because of its restriction to pastors.

Some may argue that all leaders of ministries (hospitality, community groups, mercy, etc.) should be elders. In other words, all men who are leading ministries must be elders, and women cannot lead ministries because they're not elders. If a church opts for this approach, it should be aware that unless it has a large number of elders, and unless their number is ever increasing, the church will severely limit its reach and its ability to expand its ministry to encompass a growing number of people. The alternative is for the church to have a large number of deacons, with the number of deacons increasing, and limit this diaconate to men only. This approach reflects the church leadership structure (1b) from above:

(1b) churches have a plurality of elders and a plurality of deacons: moreover, even though there is a clear distinction between elders, who must be men (in accordance with 1 Timothy 2:12–15), and deacons, only men can be deacons.

The difficulty of this approach is its understanding of 1 Timothy 2:12–15: Paul prohibits women from teaching and exercising authority over a man, urging them instead to remain quiet. For the reasons for his prohibition, the apostle appeals to the order of creation (v. 13, with allusion to Genesis 2:7 and 18–25) and to Eve's fall (v. 14, with allusion to Genesis 3:1–7). Paul's restrictions are two: women are prohibited from communicating sound doctrine and leading the church. Clearly, this restriction is not complete, encompassing all occasions. Indeed, women prophesy and pray when the church is gathered together for worship (1 Corinthians 11:5), and women teach other women (Titus 2:3–5). But in the context of the church's worship and at its highest level of authority, women are not to teach or exercise authority.

Paul's prohibition raises the question: From whom are women to learn? And to whom are women to submit? He answers these questions in his next section. According to 1 Timothy 3:1–7, the church is to be taught and led by its elders. They must be able to teach (1 Timothy 3:2) and bear the responsibility to communicate sound doctrine (1 Timothy 5:17; Ephesians 4:11). And they must be able to lead (1 Timothy 3:5) and bear the responsibility to lead (1 Timothy 5:17; 1 Peter 5:1–5). Accordingly, all women and all non-elder men are to learn from and submit to the pastors of the church. These leaders are to be qualified men and not women.

Accordingly, if a church insists that all its ministries leaders are elders, it seems that it has significantly expanded the reach of this office beyond its scriptural framework. Alternatively, if a church insists that all its leaders are deacons, and it restricts this office to men only, it seems that has significantly expanded the prohibition beyond its scriptural framework.

In summary, pastors are accompanied in ministry by deacons and deaconesses. Elders teach, lead, pray, and shepherd, and deacons and deaconesses serve in all other ministries. Together, these two groups of leaders share the responsibilities and burdens of the church, and together they equip the church to mature and to multiply. Importantly, God has designed this leadership and service structure to provide fully for the church of Jesus Christ to be all that it is called to be!

PRINCIPLES

QUESTIONS THAT MUST BE ANSWERED

What Is the Difference Between Members and Deacons?

Given that all Christians are called to serve, what's the difference between men and women serving in the church and men and women serving as deacons and deaconesses in the church? The expectation is that all members regularly serve, passionately, powerfully, and sacrificially. As they do, and they prove themselves blameless (1 Timothy 3:13) in both life and ministry, they are publicly recognized as qualified men and women leading ministries, and the church acknowledges them officially as deacons and deaconesses. Because this office is not reserved for a certain number of elite people, an increasing number of members

> **The expectation is that all members serve regularly, passionately, powerfully, and sacrificially.**

should be moving toward recognition as deacons and deaconesses.

For example, Hudson and Anni become members of the church and eagerly begin to serve in the hospitality ministry. They serve well in welcoming newcomers, connecting them with hospitable members, accompanying them to drop off their kids to kids' ministry classrooms, and following up the next week with an email or phone call to inquire how the church can further serve them. In this way, they serve like all the other members of the church should.

In time, not only do Hudson and Anni prove themselves capable in extending hospitality; they strengthen that ministry by introducing new elements, smoothing out the process of meeting and greeting newcomers, and recruiting new members to join the ministry. Furthermore, they demonstrate themselves to fulfill the qualifications of deacon. Thus, Hudson becomes a deacon and Anni becomes a deaconess of hospitality, leading other servants in this vital ministry.

Consider another example: Caleb and Ali become members of the church and immediately join a community group. When needed, they open their home to host the group. They help two of their group members to move into a new apartment, and they give financially when a community group family falls on hard times. Caleb and Ali serve like all the other members of the church should.

Eventually, the community group leaders see great potential in this couple and ask them to consider leading a community group of their own. Caleb and Ali begin discipling some of the group members, facilitate the weekly gathering when the leaders are absent, and participate in community group leaders training. They demonstrate themselves to be qualified for the office of deacon. At the appropriate time, the community group multiplies, launching a new group with this couple as its leaders. Caleb becomes a deacon and Ali becomes a deaconess of community life.

Christians are called to be faithful members of a church family. They serve the church, give generously to the church, seek the welfare of the church, and rest on the message of the church — the gospel of Jesus Christ. Every believer is commanded to engage in such participation. Moreover, the local church is dependent on such members to be a healthy and vibrant expression of Christ's body. Biblically, these members are led by the elders who love, teach, and care for them. However, without deacons to serve and care for the many needs of the church body (always under the authority and commission of the elders), the full spectrum of the work of the ministry is not possible. It is not enough to have members and elders. Deacons are vital for the health of the local body of Christ.

A caution is warranted here. There is a difference between developing leadership roles and creating a hierarchy. If careful attention is not taken, the diaconate can become a means of achieving higher status in the church. We have seen situations where the title of deacon was considered a crown to be earned rather than indicating an office of service. This is dangerous. In order to avoid this misconception, vigilance in training must include not only what a deacon is — a servant — but also what a deacon is not — a person in a position of power. A common practice to be avoided is over-using the title when referring to deacons or deaconesses. This is a sure way to create a hierarchy in your church body. We must not feel the need to call Liam "deacon" Liam and Ella "deaconess" Ella in all situations simply because they fill those roles. They ought to be known as deacons in the church, but not in such a way as to lord it over others. Though subconsciously for most, the aspiration to a greater title that leads to greater recognition and respect can be tempting. Just as the title "Dr." may be a motivation for a medical student, so too can the title "deacon" be a motivation for desiring the role. The appropriate motivation for a medical student is to aid and serve people, and the correct motivation for a deacon is to do the same in the church.

Should Deacons and Deaconesses Serve in Specific Ministries?

The short answer is yes. As these qualified men and women are leading servants in non-elder roles, they should engage in specific ministries over which they are given authority and responsibility. They are publicly recognized as deacons and deaconesses of mercy ministries, community groups, kids' ministries, hospitality, missions, bereavement ministries, and more, and they should lead others serving in those ministries.

That being said, it is certainly possible for deacons and deaconesses to change ministries. Perhaps Vaughan faithfully serves for years as a deacon of high school ministry, proving his ability to lead. When he gets married, he shifts responsibility for serving with teenagers to serving with adults and transitions to become a deacon of men's ministries. If Zoe demonstrates a well-developed competency as a leading servant in kids' ministry, but also distinguishes herself as gifted in administration and organization, she transitions to become a deaconess of children's ministry and operations. In all transitions, the congregation should be informed so they know which deacons and deaconesses are responsible for which ministries.

Should Deacons and Deaconesses Be Limited in What They Can Do?

Though needing to meet specific qualifications, and though assigned to specific ministries, deacons and deaconesses are not restricted to activities in keeping with their qualifications and assigned tasks. For example, deacons and deaconesses do not need to be able to teach, as is true of elders (1 Timothy 3:2). Just because they are not expected to have this competency does not mean that if they are able to teach, or even have the gift of teaching (1 Corinthians 12:28, 29), they are not permitted to do so. Thus, a church may use Hugo, a deacon of finance, to teach a men's Bible study. Similarly, a church may ask Ethan, a deacon of worship, to preach a sermon on worship. Likewise, deacons and deaconesses do not need to be able to shepherd the flock, as is true of elders (1 Peter 5:1–4). Just because they are not expected to meet this qualification does not mean that if they are able to care for and counsel others, or even have the gifts of exhortation and mercy (Romans 12:6–8), they are not permitted to do so. Thus, a church may rely on Chelsi, a deaconess of administration, to shepherd hurting women through tough spots in their life. Similarly, a church may encourage Everett and Guy, deacons of finance, to engage regularly in evangelistic conversations with non-Christians visiting the church. Accordingly, though deacons and deaconesses are leading servants engaged in specific ministries, they are not restricted in their activities to those ministries. Elders can and should commission them to serve in ways that are most beneficial to the body.

How Many Deacons Should a Church Have and How Long Should They Serve?

When the diaconate is a formal board with members who are nominated by some type of nominating committee, the general requirement is that there be more candidates nominated than positions being presented so the congregation can make a choice for the limited number of deacons.

On the other hand, when the diaconate consists of the leading servants in non-elder level roles within ministries of the church, a limitation on the number of deacons and deaconesses is unnecessary — and even dangerous. All qualified and gifted men and women are essential for the health and multiplication of the church; indeed, without them, the church would suffer in terms of wellness and mission. Accordingly, as the church grows, members who demonstrate solid character and serving competencies should be entered into the deacon(ess)-in-training process and, upon completion of it, should be installed as deacons and deaconesses. This latter option is preferred. There is no biblical reason to treat the office of deacon as a formal board who are nominated and elected to their post. A limitation to the number of, as well as term limits on, deacons are at best, unnecessary, and at worst, dangerous.

The above position advising against term limits may still raise considerable concern about what to do with deacons and deaconesses who are not serving well. With term limits in place, a church has an established structure by which it can get out from under the poor ministries of some of its servants. Without such limits, removing deacons and deaconesses who are underperforming becomes more complicated. Thus, it is advisable that the church establish some type of evaluation for all its leaders — elders, deacons, and deaconesses alike. Focusing on the diaconate, the elders bear the responsibility to conduct regular evaluation of those who serve in this office. Diaconal qualifications and competencies (1 Timothy 3:8–11) are the metrics by which deacons and deaconesses are assessed. Check out Appendix 3 for a list of questions that should prove helpful when evaluating deacons and deaconesses.

PROCESS

THE DEVELOPMENT OF DEACONS

The Course of Development

Not every church has deacons and deaconesses. Many of those who do, lack a suitable process for developing new ones. In either case, a process is required to recognize, identify, equip, and resource men and women in the church to this role. A sample process follows:

Nomination by a ministry leader: men and women who demonstrate a servant's heart and engage in fruitful service in the church, are identified as candidates for the diaconate. In many cases, ministry leaders — elders/pastors, deacons, and deaconesses — make this initial identification. Additionally, other members, intuitively acknowledging servant-hearted and fruitful members through comments such as "she is such a selfless servant," may contribute to this identification.

Initial conversation to assess interest in role: church leaders engage with these potential deacons and deaconesses in order to discern their desire, availability, and commitment. Some members may be eager to serve in this way, others may sense that the timing is not right, while others may not want to serve in this way. The focus now turns to those who want to serve in the diaconate.

Invitation to enter into the deacon(ess)-in-training process: church leaders extend an invitation to potential servants to begin the process. It is important to underscore that completion of the training does not guarantee that those who enter the process will become deacons and deaconesses (church leaders may assess that these potential servants are not qualified or are not yet ready to serve in this way), nor that they must necessarily serve in this office upon completion of the process (these potential servants themselves may assess that they are not qualified or are not yet ready to serve).

Entrance into the education phase: the church may develop its own deacon(ess)-in-training process, or it may use already existing curriculum like Alexander Strauch, *The New Testament Deacon: The Church's Ministry of Mercy* (Lewis and Roth, 1992), which takes the position that 1 Timothy 3:11 refers to the wives of deacons; or Benjamin Merkle, *40 Questions about Elders and Deacons* (Kregel, 2008), which presents both positions. Essential components of this preparation include:

(1) *A clear understanding of the gospel and an ability to communicate it*: A gospel-centered church is characterized by all its leaders — pastors/elders,

deacons, and deaconesses — and all its members embracing the gospel, living out the implications of the gospel, and communicating the gospel to others. The ability to teach (like that of an elder) is not in view here. Rather, this communication is the ability to explain the good news.

(2) *A grasp of basic Christian doctrine and practice*: Though the pastors/elders of the church bear the ultimate responsibility for sound doctrine and right practice, deacons and deaconesses as public servants "must hold the mystery of the faith with a clear conscience" (1 Timothy 3:9). They are therefore responsible to help pass on and "to contend for the faith that was once for all delivered to the saints" (Jude 3).

(3) *A life characterized by the fullness of the Holy Spirit, faith, and wisdom*: Deacons and deaconesses are expected to consciously and continually obey the command to "be filled with the Spirit" (Ephesians 5:18), yielding moment by moment to the Spirit's control, submitting themselves to the Spirit's will. Accordingly, they will be described as people who are "full of the Spirit" (Acts 6:3) in terms of the overall tenor of their life. Moreover, they are expected to be men and women who believe the promises of God, trusting him as Lord, who will provide all the resources needed to serve fruitfully in their ministry. Accordingly, they will be described as people who are "full of faith" (Acts 6:5). Furthermore, deacons and deaconesses are

expected to mine Scripture and heed it, ask the Lord for wisdom, and develop the mind of Christ.

Specific competencies relative to one's area of service: First and foremost, wherever possible, deacons and deaconesses with spiritual gifts and skills needed for fruitful engagement in the various areas of service should be serving in those areas. As there are many such service areas, the following is only illustrative:

(1) For community group leaders, these competencies include skills at gathering, leading, praying, facilitating, and multiplying one's group in terms of discipleship, care, and mission.

(2) For hospitality, these skills include meeting, warmly welcoming, accompanying, giving directions clearly, assisting patiently, and joyfully serving newcomers, bothered and beleaguered members, and embarrassing and/or potentially dangerous emergencies.

(3) For men's and women's ministries, these proficiencies include teaching the Bible, communicating sound doctrine, organizing and leading conferences and retreats, forming strong relationships, and caring for participants.

(4) For mercy ministries, these abilities include expressing compassion, valuing all people as image bearers of God, shunning the creation of

dependency, and avoiding burnout due to the exhaustive nature of caring for others.

Assessment of character qualifications and testing of service competencies: Throughout the training process, its leaders should carefully watch the participants, engage them in conversation regarding their strengths and weaknesses, develop specific steps for maximizing strengths and making progress in weaknesses, encourage them, and disciple them to become more fruitful servants. As noted earlier, this assessment is of both the character and competencies of the participants.

Successful completion of the deacon(ess)-in-training process: The above assessment should be part of a final evaluation of the participants in (1) determining their suitability to be recommended to the elders for installation to the diaconate, (2) urging them to continue to work on specific areas so the recommendation can be made in the future, or (3) removing from consideration.

Approval by the elders: Ultimately, the pastors/elders will assess the candidates put forward by the leaders of the deacon(ess)-in-training process. They may approve moving forward with the candidates, put them on hold, or remove them from consideration.

Installation as deacons/deaconesses during a congregational meeting: The step of public recognition is important. The congregation must know its servant-leaders and the ministries in which they serve. It also serves as an important teaching moment for the rest of the church—both members and attenders. The elders would do well to spend an extended period of time (5–10 minutes) to explain the role of deacon and how it functions in the body of Christ for the health of the church.

The Transition from Deacon Board to Elder Plurality

How can a church with a traditional polity of a solo pastor and board of deacons transition to a polity featuring a plurality of elders and a plurality of deacons and deaconesses? We think the best way to answer such a question is to share Gregg's experience of going through just such a transition.

When I (Gregg) became Chairman of the Board of Deacons at Hinson Memorial Baptist Church in Portland, Oregon, I inherited a traditional governance structure of a solo pastor (Bruce) with a dozen men composing a deacon board. Bruce was the only pastor/elder, and the board members functioned in some ways as elders and in other ways as deacons. I had been reading and teaching about the New Testament's model of a plurality of elders, a pattern that exists without exception in every church for which the New Testament presents a snapshot of its leadership structure. As I have written elsewhere:

> Scripture always presents a church being led by a plurality of elders ("council of elders"; 1 Timothy 4:14), never a solo leader. For example, at the end of their missionary journey, Paul and Barnabas appointed elders (plural) in each of the newly planted churches (Acts 14:23). Other examples of a plurality of elders include

the churches of Jerusalem (Acts 15:2, 4, 6, 22, 23), Antioch (11:30), Ephesus (20:17, 28; 1 Timothy 5:17), Crete (Titus 1:5), and "the Dispersion" (James 1:1; 5:14).[1]

With Bruce's support, I developed an approach to move Hinson Church to move its current polity to one that reflected the biblical pattern.

I knew that the key to this future transition would be for the board to become convinced by Scripture itself that this new pattern was indeed the way Hinson Church should be governed. Accordingly, in addition to our regular third Tuesday evening of the month board meeting (in which we handled the business of the church), I instituted a regular first Tuesday evening of the month Bible study and prayer time for the deacons. From 6:30 to 7:00 p.m. we ate pizza together, then from 7:00 until whenever (sometimes 9:00, sometimes 10:00 or later; at times the deacons did not want to leave!) we read and studied one chapter of the Bible, accompanied by application and prayer for our church. We began with 1 Timothy 1, then 1 Timothy 2, then 1 Timothy 3, and made our way through the other Pastoral Epistles and James over the course of the next two years.

What became evident through our study was that Hinson Church was improperly governed and needed to transition to a plurality of elders instead of a solo pastor and board of deacons. Because Scripture was the guide to our growing understanding, even the strongest challenges — "but we've

---

[1] Gregg R. Allison, *50 Core Truths of the Christian Faith: A Guide to Understanding and Teaching Theology* (Grand Rapids: Baker, 2018), 309–310.

never done it this way before!" and "a plurality of elders is Presbyterian, not Baptist!" — weren't insurmountable.

Even as Bruce left to take another pastorate and I left Western Seminary to join the faculty of The Southern Baptist Theological Seminary, the momentum toward a new polity continued to build. In the third year the deacons, now led by Hinson's new pastor Gary, read Alexander Strauch's *Biblical Eldership*. The fourth year was spent communicating the vision for a plurality of elders to the congregation through small groups, forums, listening sessions, Sunday school classes, and the like. Through a process of discernment of calling and competencies, the current members of the board agreed either to become the new elders or remain as deacons. The leaders rewrote Hinson's constitution and bylaws to reflect the new structure, then brought the revision to the congregation for its affirmation.

I was brought back to preach the sermon formally setting forth Hinson's vision to bring its polity in line with the Bible. (I still vividly recall one older member shaking his head during my message — not up-and-down to signal his agreement, but back-and-forth to signal his disgust — attempting to sway the congregation's vote and to discourage me. I did something I had never done before, and something I've never done after: I urgently called him out, telling him to stop shaking his head in disagreement but to listen instead! Thankfully, it worked!) When the vote was taken, only a handful of members did not affirm the new polity. Over a decade later, Hinson Church is still governed by a plurality of elders and has a plurality of deacons.

I learned many lessons from this situation. First, such a transition takes a long period of time, as people and church cultures change very slowly. I am aware of churches that have attempted to make this same transition but failed to do the necessary preparatory work. In some cases, the congregational vote has gone against the change. In other cases, the vote was favorable, but it split the church, with those voting against the change leaving in anger or feeling marginalized. It took Hinson Church four years to make the transition, and I would not have attempted to do it in any less time. Perhaps after a couple of years of considering it we could have forced a vote, maybe even winning. What would have changed, however, would have been the structure, not the people's heart and the church's culture. And it is people and culture that must undergird and precede any polity change.

> **It is people and culture that must undergird and precede any polity change.**

A second lesson is the importance of grounding such a transition in the Word of God. Slowly, month in and month out, we deacons studied and prayed over biblical texts that addressed the calling, character, competencies, and chemistry of elders, whom the New Testament always presents in terms of a plurality. I am thankful for that group of men who took Scripture seriously and wanted to obey it above everything else. Even when it challenged them by exposing Hinson's incorrect structure, they responded by grappling with the need for the church to change its polity — even when Hinson had never done it that way before. A firm biblical foundation is crucial for any change, including the transition to a new leadership structure.

A third lesson is the wisdom in clearly demarcating between elders and deacons in the church. Under Hinson's traditional polity, the members of the board at times functioned as elders and at other

A firm biblical foundation is crucial for any change.

times functioned as deacons. In such a structure, it was proper for the deacons to be qualified men only so they would not violate the scriptural instructions about male elders and prohibitions against women serving in this office. But when a church is properly structured with a clear distinction between elders and deacons, then the first office remains for qualified men only while the second office is accessible to both qualified men and qualified women.

Finally, a fourth lesson takes its cue from the real estate motto "location, location, location." For churches, especially those making major transitions, the motto must be "communication, communication, communication." In order to change its members' hearts and its culture, the leaders must clearly, simply, earnestly, and repeatedly communicate their vision, biblical foundation, rationale, transition timeline and concrete steps, and more. And good leaders solicit the congregation's wise input, carefully listening to it and make the necessary adjustments to incorporate that wisdom in the church.

The Transition from Deacon to Elder

In the case of deacons (not deaconesses), should the diaconate be viewed as a training ground or preparatory stage for them to become elders of the church? The short answer is no. Because the requirements and responsibilities of elders and deacons are significantly different, the latter office should not be seen as a stepping stone to the former office. While some deacons may possess highly developed competencies in leading and teaching, and thus may eventually become elders, many deacons do not have those abilities and thus are rightly suited to be deacons rather than elders.

Years ago, I (Ryan) served as an elder and a lead pastor at a multisite mega church. At times, though certainly not always, the diaconate functioned as an eldership stepping stone for men. Of course, many male deacons may appropriately, over time, become elders. This makes sense from a relational and spatial point of view — deacons are quite visible as they work alongside elders and develop close relationships with them — such that the elders should be attentive to those deacons who distinguish themselves in ministry. Such fruitfulness may be indicative of God's call on them to become elders, if they meet the requisite qualifications and have the required competencies.

However, in the example of my previous church, men would regularly be asked to enter into the diaconate for the very purpose of initiating the first step of their elder training process. In other words, men who were not currently serving as deacons were identified as potential future elders (for various reasons, some appropriate and some not) and, for the very reason of elder aspirations, were asked to enter into the deacon process. The diaconate was thus used as a means to an end. In one sense, the diaconate is indeed a means to an end, that of being a healthy local body of Christ that loves and serves her people well. In another sense, the diaconate ought never to be used as a means to an end, if that end is the advancing one's standing in the church.

CONCLUSION

There are many dissimilarities between first-century churches and our local churches today. The languages are different, the cultures are different, and the gatherings even look different. However, the purposes for which Paul wrote to those early churches are the same for our churches: that Christ may be proclaimed and glorified, and that his people would be a family characterized by their love for others, both inside and outside the church.

Paul's letter to a young church in Rome consists of two neatly-organized sections. The first section (Romans 1–11) consists of virtually no imperatives and little of what we typically call "practical application" (though these titles may be unhelpful as doctrine is always practical). The second section (Romans 12–16) is exceedingly practical, and the imperatives start to fly. The implication is simple: the truths of who humanity is, who God is, and what God has done for humanity will result in a changed life for those who have been given Christ's righteousness.

As Paul begins his most practical section, he immediately speaks of love between Christians:

> Love one another with brotherly affection. Outdo one another in showing honor. Do not be slothful in zeal, be fervent in spirit, serve the Lord. Rejoice in hope, be patient in tribulation, be constant in prayer. Contribute to the needs of the saints and seek to show hospitality. (Romans 12:10–13)

These four verses could be the vision statement of the diaconate. To identify, train, and commission people to cultivate an environment that looks like Romans 12:10–13 is the goal of the diaconate. Our churches may bear many differences from those in Paul's day, but God's desire for his church then is still his desire now. May we lead our churches into the love and service with which God has commissioned his church. May we love his church well and train deacons and deaconesses to do the same.

PRACTICES

APPENDICES

APPENDIX ONE

CASE STUDIES

These case studies are intended to be used by elders, deacon(esse)s, and deacon(esse)s-in-training to better understand the diaconate. By thinking through these situations and coming to a biblically-centered answer, these leaders will become more grounded in the nature, qualifications, and responsibilities of the diaconate.

Case Study #1

A number of new people in your church approach you about a concern they have. These people are from a traditional church background in which all leadership positions are held by men and all public roles are carried out by men: The pastor is a man, the deacons are men, those who distribute the elements of the Lord's Supper are men, those who lead and speak in the worship service are men (they read Scripture, pray, make announcements, lead singing), and more. Their concern is that your church incorporates women in leadership positions and employs them in public roles. They see women organizing and instructing through their visible roles in the worship service, facilitating courses on missions and mercy ministries, and asking discussion questions in community groups. In particular, they are concerned that your church's practice of using women in these ways violates 1 Timothy 2:12–14 and 1 Corinthians 14:34–35.

- How would you address this concern with these new people in your church?

Case Study #2

Tim Keller shares this story in his book, *Generous Justice*:

When I was a young pastor at my first church in Hopewell, Virginia, a single mother with four children began attending our services. It became clear very quickly that she had severe financial problems, and several people in the church proposed that we try to help her. By that time I had begun to share my doctoral research with some of the church's deacons. I pointed out that historically church deacons had given aid in exactly these circumstances. So, the deacons visited her and offered to give her church funds for several months to help her pay off outstanding bills. She happily accepted.

Three months later it came out that, instead of paying her bills with the money we had been giving her, she had spent it on sweets and junk food, had gone out to restaurants with her family multiple times, and had bought each child a new bike. Not a single bill had been paid, and she needed more money.

- How should the elders and deacons handle this situation?

Case Study #3

In your hospitality ministry, it becomes clear that some of the deacons and deaconesses are leading their ministries very well, others are not doing well (some have even become inactive), and church members who are not deacons or deaconesses are engaged very faithfully and fruitfully in serving. This confusing situation is causing tempers to fray, gossip to abound, and cynicism to poison the ministry.

- How would you address this situation?

Case Study #4

It becomes known to the elders and deacons that a particular deacon is asking people in the church to refer to him as "deacon" Mark instead of by his first name. As some people have questioned his motives, he has maintained that because he is qualified for the role and has been commissioned by the elders to the role, he thinks that it is appropriate for others to refer to him as "deacon." This has resulted in anger and hurt for both Mark and others.

- How would you counsel both Mark and the people who have argued with Mark?

APPENDIX TWO

RESOURCES FOR DEACONS AND DEACONESSES

Alexander Strauch, *The New Testament Deacon: The Church's Ministry of Mercy* (Lewis and Roth, 1992)

Benjamin Merkle, *40 Questions about Elders and Deacons* (Kregel, 2008)

Henry Webb, *Deacons: Servant Models in the Church*, updated ed. (B&H, 2001)

Thabiti M. Anyabwile, *Finding Faithful Elders and Deacons* (Crossway, 2012)

Paul Chappell, *The Ministry of a Baptist Deacon: A Handbook for Local Church Servant Leaders* (Striving Together Publications, 2010)

Marvin A. McMickle, *Deacons in Today's Black Baptist Church* (Judson, 2010)

Matt Ford, *That Deacon Book: Hopefully, the Least Boring Book You'll Ever Read about Deacons* (Lucid Books, 2017)

APPENDIX THREE

EXAMINING QUESTIONS FOR DEACON(ESS) CANDIDATES

Questions for Men and Women

After prayerful reflection of the Scriptures (Acts 6:1–7, 1 Timothy 3:8–13), prayer and self-examination, and discussion with your spouse (if applicable), please answer the following questions:

1. How long have you been a member?
2. Which passages in the Bible address deacons, and what kinds of ministry did they do?
3. After reflecting on the biblical qualifications of deacons found in 1 Timothy 3:8–13, assess how your heart and life compare to these qualifications.
4. Are there any sinful struggles overwhelming you right now in your individual life and/or with others that would keep you from serving as a deacon at this time and bring dishonor to the office of

deacon, and more importantly, bring dishonor to the gospel?

5. Are you dealing with sexual sin? Lust/Internet problems? Is this systemic/habitual or is it occasional? If married, have you confessed this struggle with your spouse?

6. How are your finances? Are you in debt? How much? How many credit cards? Is it student debt or lifestyle choices-debt?

7. How long to you plan to live here? (This question is important for students and members whose work frequently requires them to move.)

Questions for a Married Men and Women Considering the Office of Deacon(ess)

After prayerful reflection of the Scriptures (Acts 6:1–7, 1 Timothy 3:8–13) discussion with your spouse (if applicable), prayer and self-examination, please answer the following questions:

1. How is your marriage?

2. How have you grown as a result of being a husband/wife?

3. What does your husband/wife think about the decision to serve as a deacon at this time?

4. How might this decision to serve as a deacon(ess) impact your responsibilities as a husband/wife?

APPENDIX FOUR

EXAMPLE DEACON(ESS) DEVELOPMENT PROCESS

Our churches have found the chart on the following pages helpful. Feel free to use it as is or modify it for your own purposes.

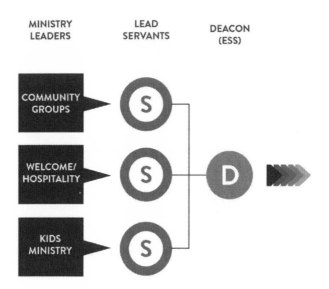

MINISTRY LEADERS   LEAD SERVANTS   DEACON (ESS)

COMMUNITY GROUPS — S

WELCOME/ HOSPITALITY — S — D

KIDS MINISTRY — S

1. IDENTIFY

- Deacon(ess) identifies a person who is a leading servant & exhibits qualities in 1 Tim. 3:8-13.

- Leading servant is given increased responsibilites in respective area.

2. TRAIN

- Deacon(ess) trains lead servant in the how & why of deacon ministry.

- Lead servent reads & studies assigned books.

- Lead servant proves to be compotent in the greater responsibilities given.

ELEDERS

DEACON-
ELECTS

MEMBERS
MEETING

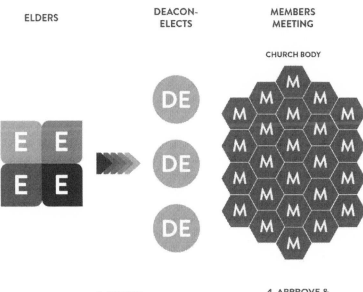

CHURCH BODY

3. REVIEW

- Deacon(ess) submits names of lead servants to Elders.

- Elders review lead servants & assess fitness for role.

- Elders inform members of deacon-elects.

- Members have opportunity to raise concerns about deacon-elects with elders.

4. APPROVE & RECOGNIZE

- Elders approve deacon-elects.

- At member meeting, the church recognizes and gives thanks for new deacons & commissions them through prayer.

ABOUT THE AUTHORS

Gregg Allison (Ph.D., Trinity Evangelical Divinity School) is Professor of Christian Theology at The Southern Baptist Theological Seminary, where he has taught since 2003. He is the author of several books and the secretary of the Evangelical Theological Society. Allison is a pastor of Sojourn Church East. He is married to Nora and they have three adult children and ten grandchildren.

Ryan Welsh (D.Min., Gordon-Conwell Theological Seminary) is the lead pastor of Redeemer Church in Bellevue, Washington and an adjunct professor of preaching and biblical studies at Corban University. He is currently a Ph.D student at The Southern Baptist Theological Seminary.

ABOUT SOJOURN NETWORK

Throughout the pages of the New Testament, and especially in the book of Acts, we observe a pattern: men and women, through prayer and dependence of God and empowered by the Spirit, are sent by God (often through suffering) to spread the Word of the Lord. As this great news of new life in Christ spread into the neighboring cities, regions, provinces, and countries, gatherings of new believers formed into local communities called churches. As these gatherings formed by the thousands in the first century, the early church — taking its cue from the scriptures — raised up qualified, called, and competent men to lead and shepherd these new congregations.

Two-thousand years later, God is still multiplying his gospel in and through his church, and the Good Shepherd is still using pastors to lead and shepherd God's people. In Sojourn Network, we desire to play our part in helping these pastors plant, grow, and multiply healthy churches.

We realize that only the Spirit can stir people's hearts and bring them into community with other believers in Jesus. Yet, by offering the pastors in our network a strong vision of planting, growing, and multiplying healthy churches and by providing them with thorough leadership assessment, funding for new churches and staff, coaching, training, renewal, and resources, we can best steward their gifts for the benefit and renewal of their local congregations.

Since 2011, our aim at Sojourn Network has been to provide the care and support necessary for our pastors to lead their churches with strength and joy — and to finish ministry well.

OTHER "HOW-TO" BOOKS

Here are the current books in the "How-To" series. Stay tuned for more.

Healthy Plurality = Durable Church: "How-To" Build and Maintain a Healthy Plurality of Elders by Dave Harvey

Life-Giving-Groups: "How-To" Grow Healthy, Multiplying Community Groups by Jeremy Linneman

Charting the Course: "How-To" Navigate the Legal Side of a Church Plant by Tim Beltz

Redemptive Participation: A "How-To" Guide for Pastors in Culture by Mike Cosper

Filling Blank Spaces: "How-To" Work with Visual Artists in Your Church by Michael Winters

*Before the Lord, Before the Church: "How-To" Plan a Child
    Dedication Service* by Jared Kennedy with Megan Kennedy

*Sabbaticals: "How-To" Take a Break from Ministry before Ministry
    Breaks You* by Rusty McKie

*Leaders through Relationship: "How-To" Develop Leaders in the Local
    Church* by Kevin Galloway

Raising the Dust: "How-To" Equip Deacons to Serve the Church by
    Gregg Allison & Ryan Welsh

.

Healthy Plurality = Durable Church: "How-To" Build and Maintain a Healthy Plurality of Elders by Dave Harvey

Have you ever wondered what separates a healthy church from an unhealthy church when they have the same doctrine (and even methods) on paper? The long-term health and durability of a church simply cannot exceed the health of her elders who lead, teach, shepherd, and pray the church forward. Therefore, building and maintaining a healthy plurality of elders is the key to durability. Yet a healthy plurality is a delicate thing working through hardship and the difficulties of relationship while pursuing the noble task of eldership. If you wish to grow deeper in your theology of eldership to lead with a healthy, biblical vision of plurality, then this is your "How-To" guide.

Life-Giving-Groups: "How-To" Grow Healthy, Multiplying Community Groups by Jeremy Linneman

Cultivate life-giving, Christ-centered communities. After many years of leading small groups and coaching hundreds of small group leaders, pastor and writer Jeremy Linneman has come to a bold conviction: Community groups are the best place for us — as relational beings — to become mature followers of Christ. This short book seeks to answer two questions: How can our community groups cultivate mature disciples of Christ? And how can our groups grow and multiply to sustain a healthy church? Whether you are new to community groups or tired from years of challenging ministry, *Life-Giving Groups* is a fresh, practical invitation to life together in Christ.

Charting the Course: "How-To" Navigate the Legal Side of a Church Plant by Tim Beltz

Planting a church? It's time to plot the course toward legal validity.
Church planting is overwhelming enough before dealing with the legal and business regulations of founding a church. *Charting the Course* is for anyone, at any experience level to learn how to navigate the legal side of planting a church.

Redemptive Participation: A "How-To" Guide for Pastors in Culture by Mike Cosper

Our culture is confused. And so are we. It's not just you or them. It's all of us. But we can move past confusion and into a place of careful discernment. *Redemptive Participation* brings awareness to the shaping forces in our current culture and how to connect these dynamics with our teaching and practice.

Filling Blank Spaces: "How-To" Work with Visual Artists in Your Church by Michael Winters

In the beginning, the earth was empty. Blank spaces were everywhere. *Filling Blank Spaces* addresses a topic that usually gets blank stares in the church world. But Winters is a seasoned veteran of arts ministry and has developed a premier arts and culture movement in the United States, without elaborate budgets or celebrity cameos. Instead, this guide gives a "How-To" approach to understanding visual art as for and from the local church, steering clear of both low-brow kitsch and obscure couture. If you are ready to start engaging a wider, and often under-reached, swath of your city, while awakening creative force within your local church, then this book is for you.

Before the Lord, Before the Church: "How-To" Plan a Child Dedication Service by Jared Kennedy with Megan Kennedy

Is child dedication just a sentimental moment to celebrate family with "oohs and ahhs" over the babies? Or is it a solemn moment before God and a covenanting one before the local church? Kennedy explains a philosophy of child dedication with poignant "How-To" plan for living out a powerful witness to Christ for one another and before the watching world. Whether you are rescuing various forms of child dedication from sentimentalism or perhaps sacrament, this book will guide you to faithful and fruitful ministry honoring God for the gift of children while blessing your church.

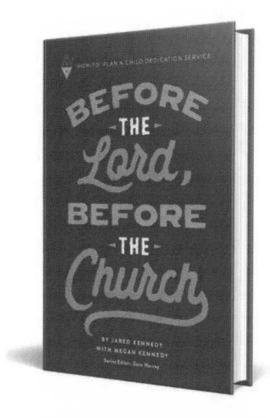

Sabbaticals: "How-To" Take a Break from Ministry before Ministry Breaks You by Rusty McKie

Are you tired and worn out from ministry? Isn't Jesus' burden supposed to be light? In the pressure-producing machine of our chaotic world, Jesus' words of rest don't often touch our lives. As ministry leaders, we know a lot about biblical rest, yet we don't often experience it. The ancient practice of sabbath provides ample wisdom on how to enter into rest in Christ. *Sabbaticals* is a guide showing us how to implement Sabbath principles into a sabbatical as well as into the ebb and flow of our entire lives.

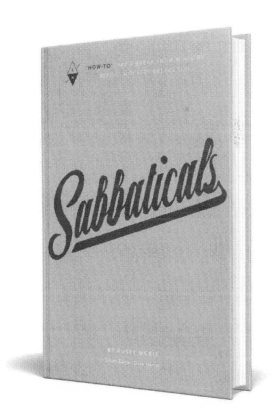

Leaders through Relationship: "How-To" Develop Leaders in the Local Church by Kevin Galloway

The church needs more godly leaders. But where do they come from? Some people read leadership books in a season of rest and health. But if we're honest, most often we read leadership books when we're frazzled, when we see the problems around us but not the solutions. If you're feeling the leadership strain in your church, let Kevin Galloway show you a way forward, the way of Jesus, the way of personally investing in leaders who then invest in other leaders—because making an intentional plan to encourage and train leaders, is not a luxury; it's mission critical, for your health and the health of your church.

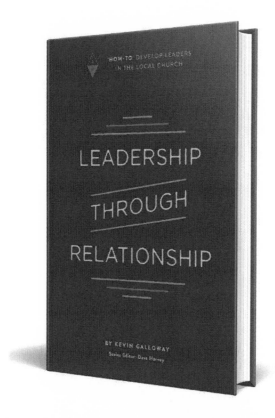

Raising the Dust: "How-To" Equip Deacons to Serve the Church by Gregg Allison & Ryan Welsh

How we organize our churches might seem insignificant, but it's not. In his letter to the church in Rome, the apostle Paul climbs great, theological mountains. But he also explores the valleys where we live our lives. Love one another with affection, he writes. Outdo one another in showing honor, he writes. Contribute to the needs of the saints and show hospitality. This is the calling of all Christians. And God intends that deacons lead the way. How is your church doing? *Raising the Dust* will help you better understand who deacons are, what God expects them to do, and how they bless the body of Christ.

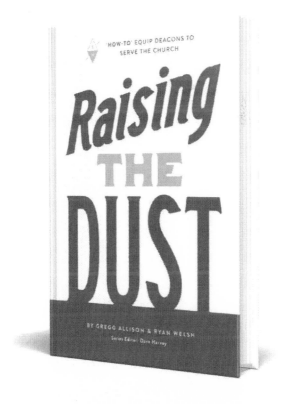

SOJOURN NETWORK "WHITE PAPERS"

Sojourn Network is committed to rigorous, biblical thinking about topics that matter. Our online Sojourn Network store (www.sojournnetwork.com/store) has "white papers" that are free to download.

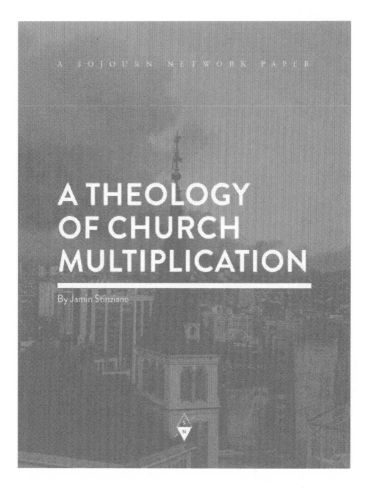

Visit www.sojournnetwork.com/store to download this resource for free.

A SOJOURN NETWORK PAPER

TO REST IS HUMAN:

ESCAPING EXHAUSTION BY TRUSTING, STOPPING, AND ENJOYING

By Daniel Montgomery

Visit www.sojournnetwork.com/ store to download this resource for free.

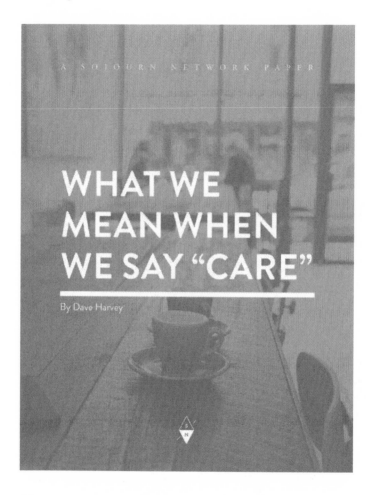

Visit www.sojournnetwork.com/store to download this resource for free.

A SOJOURN NETWORK PAPER

WHAT "NETWORK" MEANS TO US

By Dave Harvey

Visit www.sojournnetwork.com/store to download this resource for free.

Visit www.sojournnetwork.com/store to download this resource for free.

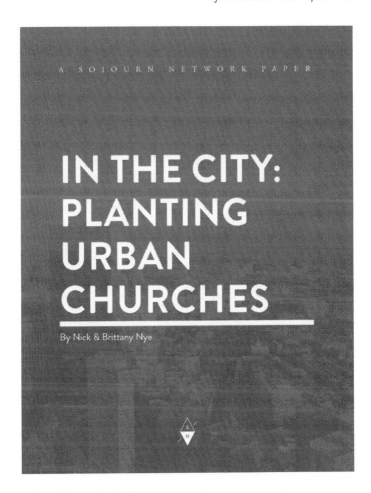

Visit www.sojournnetwork.com/store to download this resource for free.

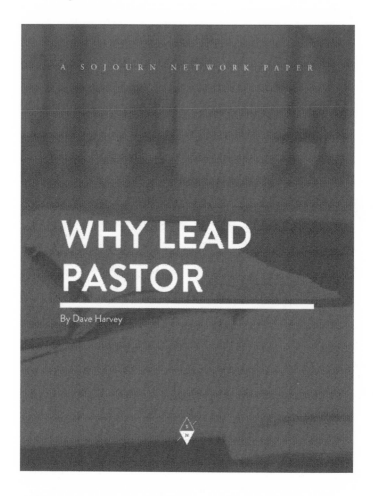

A SOJOURN NETWORK PAPER

WHY LEAD PASTOR

By Dave Harvey

Visit www.sojournnetwork.com/store to download this resource for free.

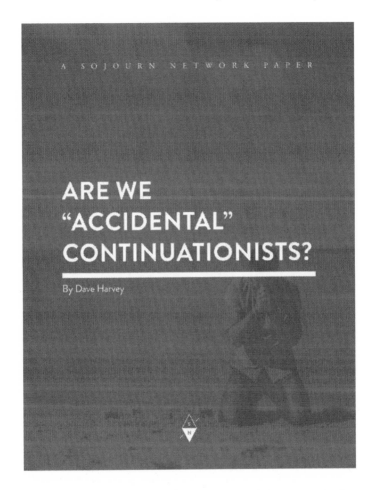

A SOJOURN NETWORK PAPER

ARE WE "ACCIDENTAL" CONTINUATIONISTS?

By Dave Harvey

Visit www.sojournnetwork.com/store to download this resource for free.

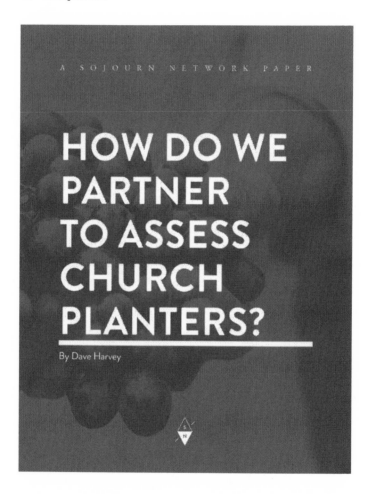

Visit www.sojournnetwork.com/store to download this resource for free.

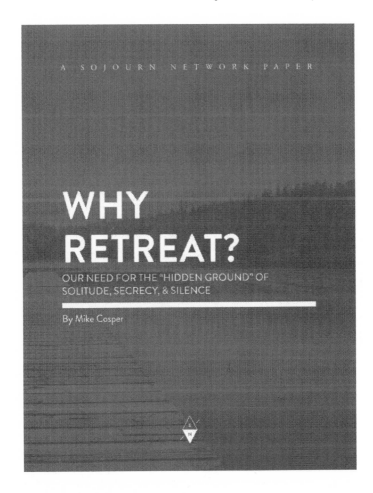

Visit www.sojournnetwork.com/store to download this resource for free.

Made in the USA
Columbia, SC
13 April 2019